Finger to HEAVEN

45

56

18-

47

paper wreaths   Friendship Wheel

100   1482   44   74

'Empty chair'   outhouse

53   34   154   Birthday Cake   154   51

Filled H2O Goblit   "READ Genesis 20-22 in C'well STUDY BIBLE"   Lyre   Anchor with ARMS

129   47   95   4.   86   58   58

Ornamented Coat hanger   sucked eggs   Cinder block   mop & Extension cord   Ceramic basket

76   83   1657   132   143   153

BARKER   SUTTON   JONATHAN M. CROWE AUG. 21, 1975 AUG. 21, 1975

plastic 6-pack holler   DAngling Conversation

"Jesus called & my darling Sugarbabe answered"

Lincoln, NM

May 16, 1992

DEAREST DWIGHT—

IT'S NEVER TO EARLY
TO PLAN FOR THE HEREAFTER—
ESPECIALLY
NOW THAT
YOU ARE 40!...

— WITH LOVE FROM SOMEONE WHO
HAS MADE IT TO THE OTHER SIDE—
(SO TO SPEAK!!)

XOXOXO,
Julie

SCORING IN HEAVEN

Gravestones and Cemetery Art of the American Sunbelt States

PHOTOGRAPHS AND TEXT BY

LUCINDA BUNNEN

AND

VIRGINIA WARREN SMITH

FOREWORD BY SUSAN KRANE

An Aperture Book

ISBN: 0-89381-474-1
Library of Congress Catalog Card Number: 90-085692

Designed by Joyce Kachergis
Typeset by Marathon Typography Service, Inc.
Printed and bound in Japan by Dai Nippon

Aperture Foundation, Inc. publishes a periodical, books, and port-
folios of fine photography to communicate with serious photographers
and creative people everywhere. A complete catalogue is available
upon request. Address: Aperture, 20 East 23rd Street, New York, NY
10010.

Distributed to the general book trade by Farrar, Straus and Giroux,
New York

FIRST EDITION

PREFACE

When we began looking seriously at grave ornaments and markers and started to find things like a baby crib, a bird cage, a fresh chocolate cake, and a six-foot Styrofoam Bugs Bunny among the usual tasteful square stones inscribed with family names, we realized that we had stumbled into unfamiliar terrain—a place, maybe the *only* place, where some people felt free to make their deepest feelings public.

As we photographed, we thought a lot about the people who had made what we were recording: their values, their taste, their sense of humor, their feelings for the departed. For the most part, we concluded, they were ordinary people, the kind of people who, as Tom Meyer puts it, built the pyramids and usually paid their taxes.

What they wrote, made, bought, or gathered to decorate the graves was what most truly expressed their feelings of respect, family pride, and grief. The candor, humor, and tenderness that these tributes reflect testifies to the human spirit's ability to transcend loss and separation. Many of the decorations are heartbreaking. Many others strike us as funny, and were clearly meant to.

All of the people involved, unaware as they were of their contribution, shared with us in the making of this book.

L . B .

V . W . S .

Myrtle Springs, TX

CONTENTS

Bristol, VA

FOREWORD
Striking Out: Another American Road Show

"Seeing the country," they call it, in earnest. The trip Out West—Yellowstone, the Grand Canyon, the Great Salt Lake; the jaunt through picturesque New England to watch the fall foliage (as if it changed before your very eyes); or the requisite California vacation—the Giant Sequoias, Disneyland, Homes of the Stars, MGM Studios, maybe even the La Brea Tar Pits. We know all too well those standard Triple-A Triptiks, the monumental family vacation taking-of-America, the many routes of our quest for the national grail. But what's *this* tour of the sunny South? It's decidedly not the usual Chamber of Commerce, postcard perspective of America, although these images indeed often share a similar prepackaged symbolic grandeur that also, unwittingly, seems to veer to the far sides of the sublime and the ridiculous. This alternative, aberrant Southern road show, however, largely forsakes the momentous and the heroic. It follows instead a trail of small, out of the way, often eccentric monuments to ordinary lives and routine voyages: gravestones. Footnotes to individuals. Lives looked at in retrospect. Death as a travelogue.

And so, as Lucinda and Ginny set out on their odyssey, they became both journeyers and documentarians. Traipsing through others' lives became a major part of their own. Their whole endeavor assumed a kind of pioneering, wagon-trail spirit: novice campers with puppy and 1960's counterculture vehicle-of-choice take off across the bottom register of America. They had not necessarily gone to look for an affirmation of life, or for the past, or even—for that matter—for an understanding of death. Rather, it seems they were looking for the thin interface between those passages, for a telling bit of humanity to capture, forever, in the limbo of photographic stasis. Their effort was itself monumental—and obsessive, as I discovered when I first was invited over to view a large basement room full of proof sheets and prints. All were organized, lovingly, by category: some were assembled into rough storyboards propped on an easel. This was truly not just a project but a campaign.

Cemeteries are pieces of perpetual (and tantalizing) alienation, points of communion that are forever thwarted by silence, separation, and inaccessibility. Perhaps they epitomize the ultimate frustration of loss, that precious melancholy of reaching out to the unreachable beloved: or perhaps they hold for us the promise of ultimate satisfaction, the opportunity to fashion the dead in our memories, in images no longer accountable to any reality but that of our own idealized, comforting imaginings.

What Bunnen and Smith's images give us is really not a vision of what it means to "score in heaven": they give us, instead, cryptic tales of what it means to survive life, and to triumph while doing so. Their photographs record vernacular biographies—from that of Cecil R. Adair, the "Gorilla" truck driver with wild sideburns, to the sage B. P. "I told you I was sick" Roberts of Key West, Florida. Some of these images *are* stern and sobering. Most, however, forego the somber, melodramatic tone of mourners' hermetic rituals. They reflect, rather, ways of waving goodbye to the dearly departed, ways of marking their death with a bit of their life to tide them (and undoubtedly us) over.

The South is still a different place, in spite of the ever-present shopping malls and franchise strips that make it appear at times just like anywhere else you've ever been. I used to spend time in a small cemetery in Miller, Indiana, where I grew up, daydreaming among plain Midwestern, weathered headstones of the early inhabitants of what used to be an outpost between the settlements at Fort Dearborn and Detroit, along Lake Michigan. The modest inscriptions told stark stories of life in the dunes that fed my romantic, adolescent, and anti-urban imagination. That place, tucked behind a houseboat factory and the South Shore railroad tracks, gave life to old ghosts and forged a sense of rootedness and of history more real than what they could ever hope to give us in school. Years later I tramped with an old college friend through a seventeenth- and eighteenth-century cemetery on a hilltop near Rockport, Massachusetts, where omnipresent, vexing winged Deaths terrified and admonished the living with Puritan force from every gravestone: an illustrated *Scarlet Letter*. Very different voices, though, come from these Southern images—louder voices, embellished songs, evoked but hauntingly withheld. What do these graves, in their decorated silence, say about the lives they mark—about the spirit, endurance, and celebrations of the families and the communities they describe?

Shortly after Ginny asked me to "write something for the front of the book," I was driving around with the radio tuned to FM 88, the Voice of Georgia State. Some neo-hard rocker was blasting out the refrain "I don't want to be buried in a pet cemetery; I don't want to live my life [long pause] over again." A psychic frequented by many in the Atlanta art community once told me that she strongly suspected a man I was seeing had been my sister in a former life. *Scoring in Heaven* pictures for us both of these extreme views of death—the desire for the blackness of the finite as well as the quixotic, often humorous paths of infinity incarnate. But mostly these images offer up a much more comfortable range of options in between. And, perhaps unconsciously, they suggest that just maybe, yes, you *can* take it with you . . .

SUSAN KRANE,
Curator of Twentieth-century Art,
High Museum of Art, Atlanta, Georgia

INTRODUCTION

Scoring in Heaven started by accident—the result of an impromptu picnic in a cemetery on the outskirts of Atlanta one August afternoon ten years ago. There, between bites of tuna salad, we discovered two curious floral displays—an empty picture frame made of Styrofoam and tulle, and a plastic telephone with a dangling receiver and the epitaph "Jesus Called." We photographed both.

Several months later, Lucinda included these pictures in an exhibition. The viewers' reaction surprised us. Even people who claimed to be graveyard aficionados had never seen anything like the empty picture frame or the dangling phone. In response to their response, we planned a few day trips to see what else might be out there. We didn't have any plan except to drive the back roads and be home by dark.

Being artists, rather than anthropologists or folklorists, our idea of methodology was intuition, chance, and luck. But, as we began to see more graves, we felt it was important to document what we were seeing. Keeping track of what was where also seemed like a good idea, so we started a card file with a card for each cemetery on which we recorded every frame shot there. (By the time we finished the project, the file had 677 cards listing over 13,000 negatives.) I kept the card file, Lucinda kept a journal.

In November we began to plan a five-month road trip. Lucinda bought a flesh-colored VW camper, which we named "the Burro" in homage to the Rolling Stones' song "Beast of Burden." Neither of us had ever camped before.

In early December we took the Burro on a three-day test run to Alabama and Mississippi. The following entries from Lucinda's journal reflect some of the highlights of that trip.

November 30, 1979
  Temperatures in the low 20's. No electricity, no water.
  Serenaded until 4 a.m. by pack of howling dogs.
December 1, 1979
  Spent night at Bob's Campground, which turned out to be an abandoned gas station.
December 2, 1979
  Camped at Lake Lurleen. Coldest night yet.
  Sheer misery. None of the camping equipment works.
  We are freezing. Even medicinal Scotch does little to help.

Despite this grim beginning, we had seen enough in the Alabama cemeteries to convince us to go ahead with the trip. We realized that we desperately needed to rethink our van-outfitting strategy if we were going to survive for five months in this vehicle, which Lucinda's sister described as being "smaller than your guest bathroom."

Our first acquisition was an Old English Sheepdog puppy. (We were at the mall looking at luggage. The luggage store was next to the pet store . . .) Daisy was the emaciated runt of the litter, had mange, and was hyperactive. Lucinda remembers her as being "adorable—appealing to all who saw her, including us." Apparently her memory is accurate, because Daisy became part of our team.

We had a carrier made for the top of the van by a sailboat outfitter (it leaked like a sieve). We bought a catalytic heater (which couldn't be left on at night in a closed van), a portable TV (there seldom was decent TV reception), and a gun. Most of these proved to be mistakes, along with a box of books that I had collected over the years but never had time to read (including a complete set of

Proust). Another mistake was a pair of pith helmets that we wore once, then discarded because we couldn't photograph and laugh that hard at the same time.

We anticipated shooting lots of film, so we opted for 35 mm cameras—2 Leicas and a Canon AE-1. We bulk-loaded black & white film and developed it in motels along the way. So in addition to our clothes, camping equipment, books, cameras, and dog supplies, we also took gallon jugs, chemicals, changing bags, 8-reel tanks, & thermometers—a rolling darkroom.

We had only 48 film cassettes, so every time we finished exposing those rolls we would have to check into a motel to develop film to free the cassettes for reloading. Each roll had to stay in sequence throughout loading the tanks, developing, washing, drying, and sleeving so that it would still match the card file.

Our system for deciding where to go was to meander. The result was 26,000 miles of driving on back roads that were often indistinguishable from arroyos or cattle paths. We found most of the cemeteries along these roads or by asking people where we could find them. We quickly learned that "Go through four stop signs" can also mean a 4-way stop.

The campgrounds were an endless source of culture shock, particularly the bathrooms, which varied enormously in cleanliness and facilities but were always a common ground among campers. A certain bond develops quickly among strangers who are brushing their teeth together.

In addition to photographing we tried to see whatever else was in the area—the Grand Ole Opry, reptile farms, wax museums, the Grand Canyon, Shark Institute, even a taping of "Laverne and Shirley" at Paramount Studio. We survived prairie fires, dust storms, snow, hail, sleet, and each other. In May we came back to Atlanta for 6 weeks of much needed R & R.

When we went back out in late June, we thought we knew exactly what to take and what to leave behind. One "essential" was a set of Evelyn Wood Reading Dynamics tapes, which we valiantly attempted to do every morning until Lucinda dropped the tape recorder into a swamp in the middle of a "push-down drill."

The summer of 1980 was one of the hottest on record, and we traveled without air-conditioning, our rationale being that we would be less likely to get out to photograph if the van were cool. Remarkably, we were still speaking when we came home in late July.

We spent the month of August assembling a book presentation. Our system for organizing the material was based on about a dozen general categories—"boxes," "crosses," "cameos," "mounds and tombs," etc. We selected the most interesting examples of each category from our contact sheets, then cut each frame out and glued it onto an appropriately headed piece of poster board. Each frame was labeled with its identification number.

In September 1980 we went to New York with these boards and about 50 prints to call on publishers. Several nibbled, none bit. We knew from our own observations that much of what we had photographed was highly perishable. We had also learned from talking to stonecutters and cemetery personnel that the practice of decorating graves was dying out as families became more mobile and cemeteries encouraged "perpetual care" maintenance. We decided to give the material some time.

Almost ten years later, in the summer of 1989, one of the "Scoring in Heaven" images was included in *Aperture*'s "New Southern Photography: Between Myth and Reality." Jonathan Williams, founder of the Jargon Society, wrote one of the essays that accompanied that volume and subsequently contacted us about the rest of our body of work. His interest and encouragement were the catalyst that eventually brought us to Aperture. This book is the result.

Our hope, in presenting these images, is to acknowledge the creativity and resourcefulness of the people who made what we photographed.

V. W. S.

Everyday Iconography :
Telephones, clocks, chairs and wheels

Paris, TN

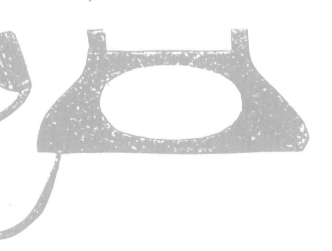

Jesus Called

White Oak Lake, AR

Calhoun, GA

Bowling Green, KY

Clock That Stopped

Nashville, TN

Empty picture frame

Canton, GA

Summerville, GA

Empty Chair

Tombstone, AZ

Nashville, TN

Train wheel

Dalton, GA

Saltville, VA

Mill Wheel
Salt Capital of the Confederacy

Glade Springs, VA

Friendship Wheel

Fish and Fowl

Big Stone Gap, VA

Gates of Heaven

Holtville, CA

Canton, GA

Columbia, SC

Live
bird
Dead
bird

Athens, LA

Jemez Indian Reservation, NM

Laurel, MS

JOSHUA THOMAS
KNOX
AUG. 28, 1978
JAN. 3, 1980
OUR DARLING

St. Mary's, GA

San Juan, NM

Big Bird

Electra, TX

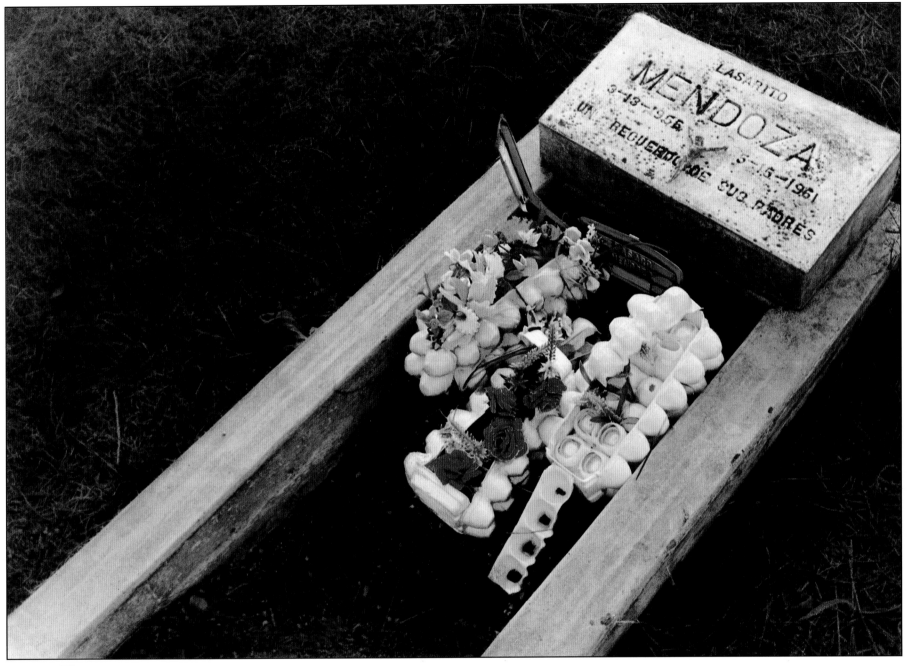

Runge, TX

Styrofoam egg cartons with blown out eggs

Canton, GA

Harlan, KY

Animals:
Fertility, Sacrifice,
and the Lord of the Jungle

Albuquerque, NM

La Costa, TX

Hohenwald, TN

Central City, KY

Turtletown, TN

ALICIA M. BURKE
SEPT. 23, 1976
NOV. 14, 1977

Big Stone Gap, VA

Family of Lamb

Elkhorn City, KY

Brevard, NC

Nuba, LA

Biloxi, MS

Birmingham, AL

Immigrant
Camel
driver for
US Army
in SW

Quartzsite, AZ

Tombs, Mounds,
and a Voodoo Queen

New Orleans, LA

Maynardville, TN

Terlingua, TX

Labadieville, LA

File box?

Tyler, TX

Point a la Hatch, LA

Terlingua, TX

Alamo, TX

Mission, TX

New Orleans, LA

Alleged tomb of Marie Laveau,
Voodoo Queen of New Orleans,
with fresh gris-gris marks

Seguin, TX

Moreland, GA

Zapata, TX

Enclosures, Gates, and Fences

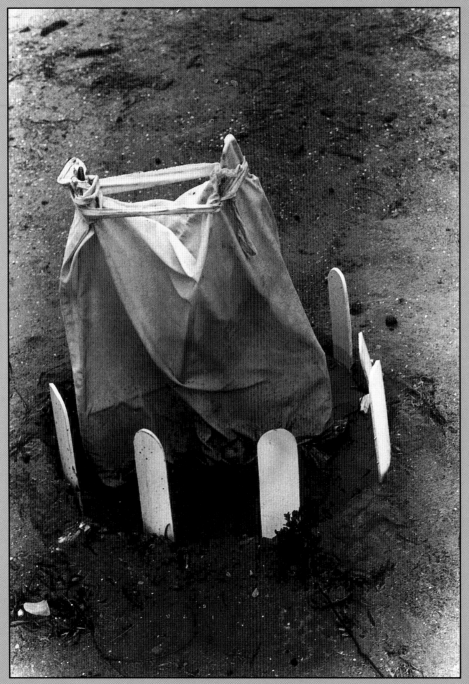

La Joya, TX

Tucson, AZ

Rancho de Taos, NM

Fredericksburg, TX

Quihi, TX

San Antonio, NM

Tombstone, AZ

Navaho Reservation, Kayenta, AZ

Las Vegas, NM

Giant basket enclosed by 6 ft. fence

Albuquerque, NM

Enclosures

Mission, TX

Totems

San Antonio, TX

Paducah, KY

White Oak, NM

Panna Maria, TX

Tennesee Williums ?

Oldest Polish Catholic
Colony in U.S. Founded
December 24, 1854.

Laredo, TX

Seguin, TX

Las Vegas, NM

Wickenburg, AZ

Socorro, TX

El Paso, TX

El Paso, TX

Tarpon Springs, FL

Tucson, AZ

Mothers. Babies, and a Father

Tombstone, AZ

Electra, TX

Cleveland, TN

Roma, TX

Baton Rouge, LA

Children died in yellow fever epidemic

New Orleans, LA

Albuquerque, NM

Newnan, GA

Nogales, AZ

Anadarka, OK

Marriage and the Family

Las Vegas, NM

Savannah, GA

Henryetta, OK

Calhoun, GA

FLORENCE CROW
JULY 2, 1915
SEPT. 27, 1974

WALTER JAMES
JAN. 7, 1915

HALL

Chickasha, OK

Florence, AL

DONNIE
FEB. 28, 1913

THIRD WIFE OF ROY SEAY

MINNIE
JUNE 16, 1888
OCT. 16, 1979

SECOND WIFE OF ROY SEAY

SEAY

Calhoun, GA

First wife buried in same plot.

Vocations / Avocations

Leesville, LA

Campbellsville, KY

Coffin maker

1885 ————— 1963

A NOBLE PURPOSE
SERVED WELL

Fox, VA

AM HOWA

Florence, AL

PHOEBE MARTINEZ

WIFE OF HANK
MARRIED OCT. 27, 1954
BORN JULY 23, 1933
DIED

TRUCK DRIVERS WIFE WAS
A TRUCK DRIVERS LIFE
WE LIVED FOR EACH OTHER

Anadarka, OK

GORILLA

CECIL R. ADAIR
DEC. 12. 1947 ~ FEB. 8. 1978

Chickasha, OK

OLIVER

HIGHWAY TO HEAVEN

SON
ARL W.
V. 15, 1951
T. 30, 1976

FATHER
GEORGE
APR. 3, 19
FEB. 8, 19

McDonald, TN

"SPEEDY"

Dryden, VA

Paris, TN

Canton, GA

Alamo, TX

Van Horn, TX

Polaroid picture is of this
gravesite with a car parked
behind it.

St. Mary's, GA

Calhoun, GA

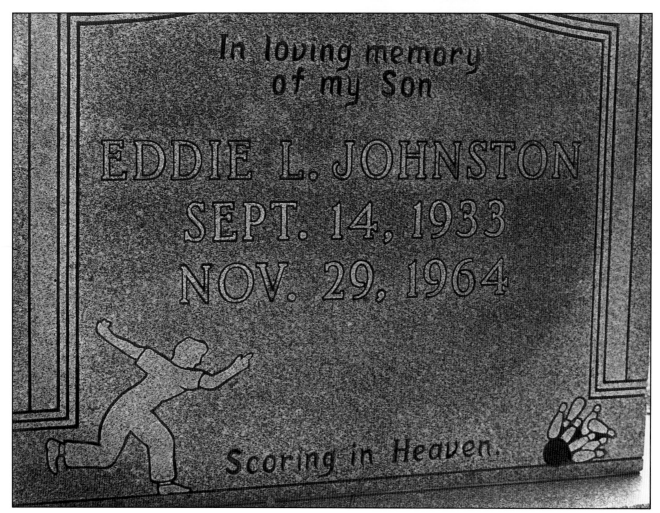

In loving memory
of my Son

EDDIE L. JOHNSTON
SEPT. 14, 1933
NOV. 29, 1964

Scoring in Heaven.

McDonald, TN

JOHN RICHARD LITTLE

APR. 26, 1939

NOV. 26, 1976

300

PEACE

Fulton, MS

Hallsville, TX

New Orleans, LA

Norton, VA

Okemah, OK

Boots and Saddles
Feathers and Shoes

Claude, TX

Skull Valley, AZ

Vulture City, AZ

Key West, FL

Tombstone, AZ

Anadarka, OK

New Orleans, LA

Yuma, AZ

Liberty Hill, TX

LILLY MAE
HALL
BORN & DIED
JUNE 30, 1952

I'LL TAKE MY FIRST
STEPS IN HEAVEN

Yuma, AZ

Ribbons and Roses

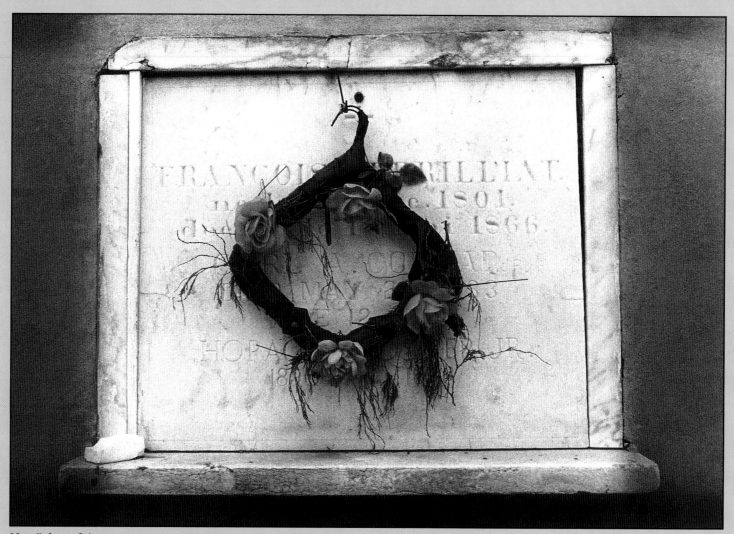

New Orleans, LA

Garciasville, TX

Robstown, TX

Papago Indian Reservation, AZ

Tarpon Springs, FL

Carville, LA

Melted Candle

Thibodaux, LA

Shrines

El Paso, TX

Leesville, LA

Saltville, VA

Mission, TX

Pinos Altos, NM

Tucson, AZ

Bourg, LA

San Elizario, TX

Rockport, LA

Fredericksburg, TX

La Rose, LA

Mission, TX

War,
Horses, Dogs, and Deer

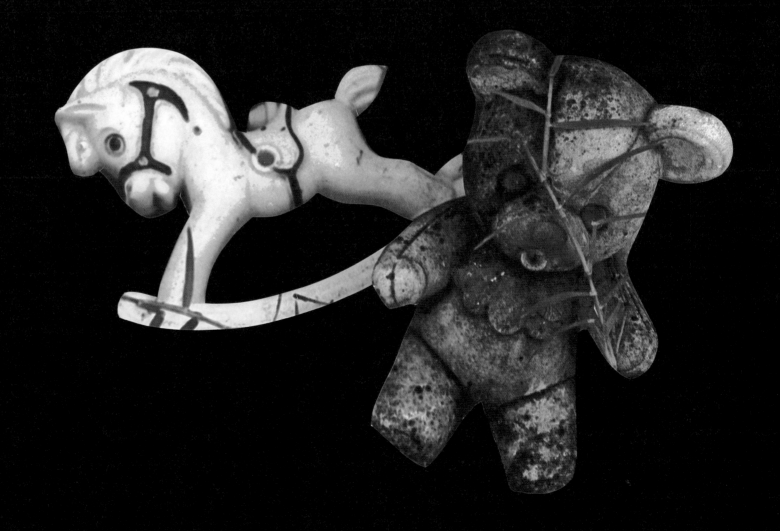

MARCHÓ ADELANTE

FRANK WORDEN
1880   1941

Hillsboro, NM

Tarpon Springs, FL

Goliad, TX

Key West, FL

ERNEST EUGENE
LOPEZ
SEPT. 16, 1945
OCT. 19, 1954

DARLING, WE MISS THEE

Memphis, TN

WAR HORSE ROGERS

Nashville, TN

Fredericksburg, TX

Norton, VA

PVT. CLIFFORD COOK
BORN AUG. 30, 1925
SERVED IN WORLD WAR II WITH THE
10TH ARMORED DIV.—3RD ARMY
LOST HIS LIFE IN BELGIUM JAN. 3, 1945

Blue Ridge, GA

Columbia, SC

Deer
buried
in human
cemetery

Key West, FL

ELFINA, OUR DEER
FLORIDA EVERGLADES
MARCH 28, 1941
CORAL GABLES, FLORIDA
SEPTEMBER 1, 1956

THE LAST HUNT

Albuquerque, NM

New Orleans, LA

Grand Couteau, LA

EVALDO

JOSE D.
BORN JUNE 10, 1914
VATRA, DORNEI, ROMANIA
DIED JAN. 1, 1971
SEEFELD, AUSTRIA
NATURALIZED U.S. CITIZEN FEB. 1951
AWARDED D.A.R. AMERICANISM MEDAL, NOV. 1960
BREEDER OF CHAMPION DOBERMANS

FR

Mt. Sterling, KY

Huntsville, AL

Gainesville, FL

Hands

Central City, KY

Smyrna, GA

כ[נ]

איש צעיר לימים משו[ש]
תורה היה והוא היה נ[?]
[א]מרי אהר[ן] מות אבין ה[?]
[?]דם בן שלשים וא[?]
שנה היה זה משה שמוא[ל]
[?]בי הכהן כמותו נפט[ר]
[?]וצא[י]ך כאור ליום הוא עב[?]

DONALD W.
CHADNEY
BORN
MAY 2 1881
D

Albuquerque, NM

Summerville, GA

Canton, GA

El Paso, TX

Louisville, KY

Beds

Resaca, GA

Phoenix, LA

Nashville, TN

Albuquerque, NM

Clint, TX

The Eternal Meal

Durham, NC

OUR DAUGHTER
ISABEL ROSE PASQUAL
AUG. 15, 1928
AUG. 23, 1956

Acoma Indian Reservation, Acomita, NM

Fresh chocolate Cake

Yuma, AZ

Tequila Bottles

Beaufort, SC

Tomatoes

Laguna Indian Reservation, Laguna, NM

SOUL FOOD
AND WHILE THEY WERE AT SUPPER JESUS TOOK BREAD, AND BLESSED
AND BROKE, AND GAVE IT TO HIS DISCIPLES, AND SAID,"TAKE AND EAT; THIS
IS MY BODY." AND TAKING A CUP, HE GAVE THANKS AND GAVE IT TO THEM,
SAYING,"ALL OF YOU DRINK OF THIS; FOR THIS IS MY BLOOD OF THE
NEW COVENANT, WHICH IS BEING SHED FOR MANY UNTO THE
FORGIVENESS OF SINS."

Titusville, FL

Tucson, AZ

Sequoyah, OK

Key West, FL

JOURNAL

1/16/80—5/9/80

1/16
Departed Atlanta. Went through torrential rain, roof carrier leaked.

1/18
Pensacola, FL. Forced to rearrange everything. Film developing equipment went up top, suitcases came down, and dog food got sorted (wet from dry).

1/24
Grand Isle, LA. Camped on beach. Truck circled our van in middle of night. Gun out for first time, but intruders left.

1/25
Bayous filled with abandoned cars. Gas station attendant explained, "It gets to be a habit."

1/26
New Iberia, LA. VWS encountered rat in bathroom during morning shower. Meanwhile I made rock Cornish hen salad in the open van and met neighbors: a bricklayer and his wife with 2 dogs that loved Daisy. Hearing of the rat, the couple raced to the bathroom to try to catch it for their boa constrictor's breakfast.

1/27
Opelousas, LA. Camped at South City Park Camp Ground, which turned out to be the Saturday night cruise strip. Fatherly park superintendent checked on us periodically until 2 a.m. to be sure we were safe.

1/29
Monroe, LA. VWS pulled hip out of joint while organizing bedding in top of van. Headed for Shreveport (80 miles away) as fast as possible to find a chiropractor, although neither of us had ever been to one before. Stopped at Hilton Hotel to ask for a reference. VWS still dressed in sleepwear (modified men's long underwear and down jacket). Embarrassed, but desperate. Would have tried a witch doctor.

Chiropractor was Ned Beattie look-alike, with white patent leather shoes and belt. Explained his empty office with no receptionist by saying he makes too much money and is trying to cut back on his practice. As he snapped her neck, her legs began to get a little closer to being the same length.

In between adjustments he told us he was 47 years old, recently divorced from his wife of 11 years, and now dates 30-year-old women. He has become a vegetarian, and has sold his Mercedes—"in Louisiana patients like it better if you have an American car." He sets goals and meditates in cemeteries. Despite his portly girth, he claims to run 2 miles a day and to have lost 40 pounds. He doesn't smoke or drink, but barmaids like him because he tips well. Most importantly, he fixed the injured back.

1/31
Mexia, TX. Barely made it to Mexia with NO gas. Passed on the only motel—"Boots and Saddles"—which was too seedy to qualify even under the heading of "indigenous."

2/2
Temple, TX. Up early, motel room too hot and dry to sleep. Saw first Roadrunner in Liberty Hill, TX, 12:45 p.m.

2/3
Pedernales Falls State Park, TX. I waded across shallow river, then hiked 6 miles with wet feet to obscure pioneer cemetery. Saw wild turkey and herd of white deer while VWS washed and deburred Daisy.

2/5
San Antonio, TX. Met people in campground bathroom with few teeth and many children.

2/6
Elm Grove, TX. Very cold. Mist rising from river. Woman saw VWS photographing her grandmother's grave and stopped, thinking her to be the cousin she hadn't seen for 30 years. She was looking for someone to talk to about her marital problems. We were there a while.

Seguin, TX. Directed to a remote cemetery by a 5-year-old girl who didn't speak much English. Drove a good while, finding nothing and no one else to ask. Finally saw a farm couple, who seemed a bit suspicious but then directed us to the right road, which turned out to be a long wagon trail that passed through 2 gates, woods and pastures, and finally ended in the cemetery. There was evidence of burning around some of the graves. All our cameras magnetized—light meters wouldn't register, shutters wouldn't trip. Went back to van and found its compass spinning. Chilling experience. Left quickly.

2/8
Corpus Christi, TX. Developed film and watched Elvis Special.

2/10
Brownsville, TX. Camped at Citrus Gardens Campground, allegedly the southernmost campground in the U.S. Usually balmy, today freezing. Most campers were fishermen, one of whom loaned us an electric heater.

2/11
Rio Grande Valley. Went to Sears and bought electric heater. Stopped along highway to watch harvest of giant carrots. Gathered some of the refuse.

Alamo, TX. Camped at Citrus Grove Campground. This one is for retired folks—shuffleboard, cards, and 3-wheeled bicycles. Each resident laid claim to an orange tree. (Our neighbor made it very clear that we were to stay on the overflow side and not pick off her side of the tree.) Dinner of oranges, grapefruit, and carrots.

2/12
Torrential rain. Residents call it "Valley Sunshine."

Mission, TX. Gas station attendant sent us to a "really spooky" cemetery—good pics.

Benson State Park was full. A nice Spanish-speaking couple said they had room for us. They let us back up into their shed, which led into the laundry and bathroom (heated!). We washed clothes, stayed dry, and had all the comforts of home. Even got invited to a potluck surprise birthday party. Declined but gave them some carrots.

2/13
Falcon Heights, TX. Met 76-year-old woman in bathroom who was living in a truck that pulls her daughter's trailer, because the daughter and her husband both smoke and she likes her privacy. She wants to go back to her part-time job, oil painting, gardening, even shoveling her own snow.

Los Ebanos, TX. Considered crossing Rio Grande on only

hand-pulled ferry across a U.S. border, but Daisy was denied entry so we didn't go.

2/14
Laredo, TX. Valentine's Day. Exchanged rocks in the rain.

2/15
Walked across border from Laredo to Nuevo Laredo. I saw a woman on the bridge with a good haircut and asked for directions to her beauty shop. Shop filled with Christmas lights and holy cards—no English, no other customers. Terrible cut. Lunch at Cadillac Bar. I forgot and drank Mexican water.

2/17
Big Bend National Park, TX. Sleet, rain, wind. Icicles hanging off back of van. I am paying price for water mistake.

2/18
Shafter, TX, a silver-mining ghost town, revived since price of silver is back up. Daisy made friends with D. J. Barley, age 4, who first appeared in only underpants with an ink drawing on his leg. Later returned with jacket, and cowboy boots on the wrong feet.

An older woman who had been sweeping dirt around her trailer came over to our van while we were fixing breakfast, leaned on her broom, and told a tale about having put her father in a nursing home. Excellent storyteller. She also told us that Shafter is the only town in Texas with no TV reception.

Valentine, TX. Photographed in cemetery where "Giant" was filmed. Passerby said, "That was the only thing that's ever happened there."

2/20
El Paso, TX. Very windy, lots of tumbleweed. We are in a war with the elements. Texas always has something to make picture-taking difficult.

2/23
Roswell, NM. Carlsbad Caverns. Camped with young couple from Santa Barbara traveling with their cross-country skis and a grill.

2/24
Truth or Consequences, NM. Camped with field mice and rabbits.

2/25
Hillsboro, NM. Met Mrs. Nowlin (90-year-old widow of railroad man who died 40 years ago), who lives alone in this ghost town with only one other family. She was dressed up, in full makeup and jewelry, when we arrived unexpectedly.

2/27
Paradise, AZ. Magnificent little town of 4 families, down long, isolated dirt road. Met woman whose dream to move there came true a month ago.

2/28
Tombstone, AZ. Commercial and hot. Named by prospector who was told he wouldn't come out of there alive. He struck gold and named his claim "Tombstone." His second claim, called "Graveyard," played out.

Dinner at Patagonia Stage Stop Restaurant. Most Western Stop in the west. Great salad bar, but I still can't eat solid food. Nice German waitress. This is where "Little House on the Prairie" is filmed.

Camped by a river in Patagonia State Park, near a group with a campfire and Willie Nelson tapes. Square-danced under full moon, many stars.

2/29

Awoke to the thundering of hundreds of blackbirds. Headed to border town of Lochiel over 100 miles of the roughest roads yet. European missionary priest came here in 1535. No road improvements since.

Nogales, AZ. Looked for Apache cemetery. Drove on wagon trails. Walked when we could no longer drive. Didn't find it.

Stopped at rest stop en route to Tucson and met retired couple from North Carolina. Husband, dressed in a white lab coat, told entertaining story of waiting in El Paso for 3 days for a new refrigerator for their RV only to watch the mechanic pound it in with a sledgehammer.

3/1–3/5

Tucson, AZ. R&R at friend's adobe house atop 350-acre cactus-covered mountain.

Daisy and Grey Wolf (resident puppy, half German shepherd, half wolf) both fell victim to jumping cholla cactus. Many hours of picking needles out of hides, gums, and tongues followed.

Invited to dinner party. Didn't have right clothes, so improvised by wearing our Mexican bedspreads.

3/7

Organ Pipe Cactus National Monument, AZ. Realized that roads marked "questionable" on the map can be anything from a dried-up creek bed to nonexistent. Camped at Yuma KOA. Palm trees and a laundry.

3/11

Beverly Hills, CA. Stayed with cousin, Michael Eisner, and his family, who were screening "Coal Miner's Daughter" that night.

3/12

Hollywood, CA. Studio tour at Paramount. Saw filming of "Laverne and Shirley." Hollywood Cemetery a bust. Pet Cemetery a bust, even with Jerry Lewis's dog buried there.

Pasadena, CA. First flat tire as we drove into filling station. Stayed in Ace Motel. Smuggled Daisy into motel despite NO PETS restriction.

3/13

Palm Springs, CA. Stopped at Saks for Sea Mud Soap. Campground featured jacuzzi, swimming pool, and many palms. Noisy expressway on other side of the wall.

3/14

Joshua Tree National Monument, CA. Had to go many miles into monument to see a Joshua tree, then saw many others later in the day, outside their monument.

3/15

Directed to Skull Valley Cemetery by drunk woman.

Jerome, AZ. Revived ghost town on mountainside. Camped in pioneer cemetery on separate hillside looking up at town and down into cottonwood grove. View of Jerome at night was spectacular under star-filled sky.

3/17

Flagstaff, AZ. St. Patrick's Day. Film developing. VWS either lost roll #76 or misnumbered.

3/18

Grand Canyon, AZ. So cold inside van overnight that drinking water in jug froze.

3/20

Canyon de Chelly, AZ. After wading down cold river to White House ruins, started over mountain toward Ft. Defiance. Mountain road turned to dirt, then ice, then sucking mud. Finally got stuck, hub-deep. Car carrying 3 Bureau of Indian Affairs employees tried to help us get out, but to no avail. They left, promising to send help if we had not called by 1 p.m. the next day. They didn't advise leaving the van alone on the reservation or having one of us stay alone with it while the other went with them for help.

After they left, a car filled with Navahos got stuck about 50 feet behind us. Seven of them jumped out, freed their car, then left without offering us any help and leaving two Navaho hitch-hiking passengers behind.

This couple was determined to walk the 24 miles to Ft. Defiance after having been stuck in their car overnight with no food or water except snow. After feeding, watering, and warming them, we realized we had them for the night. We hoped they could help push us out when the mud froze again during the night. But they settled in and pulled out a bottle of what the BIA men later dubbed "Navaho Champagne."

Tillie told us that she and Johnson (her landlord) had gone to visit her mother in Many Farms, but as the evening progressed it sounded more like she had run away from her husband.

Fortunately the 3 men from BIA returned about 10 p.m., having summoned the Navaho police. They crowded into the van to wait with all of us. We passed our bottle of Scotch around and got acquainted. The large black man, Shed, looked like Louis Armstrong and wore white patent leather shoes. Shiran, an engineer from India, had been in America only a week. Steve, a middle-aged New Mexican cowboy, looked like Jimmy Carter; he had just gotten divorced. I played the harmonica. Tillie and Johnson got drunk.

The police didn't show up. Finally, after about an hour, the BIA men went back (20 miles) and this time returned with the Navaho police in a 4-wheel-drive jeep. They pulled us out.

Drove 2½ hours back to Gallup, NM. Everything was totally covered with mud, the Burro will never recover. Checked into KOA despite offer from Steve to stay at his house. Finally bedded down at 4:30 a.m.

3/21

Gallup. Spent most of day at Steve's cleaning van and Daisy. Shed and Steve directed us to a draw to look for petrified wood. Good find.

3/22

Headed toward Albuquerque via Sky City and Laguna Pueblos. Awful dirt roads. Heater bounced loose in van and hit Daisy on the head, giving her a concussion. Went through bitter cold windstorm that almost blew us off the highway.

3/25

Madrid, NM. Met Liz and Denise, two young women from Boston fixing up mining shack. No heat or plumbing yet.

Los Cerillos, NM. "Nine Lives of Elfago Baca" was filmed here. Patricia, 27-year-old mother of 4, and her husband, the self-appointed mayor, built their own house of homemade adobe bricks. She thought Daisy would make a nice carpet.

3/27

Taos, NM. Woke to 4 inches of new snow, which made photographing difficult. Saw beautiful magpies—and adobe houses with solar heat. Taos Pueblo—snowing and very cold, bought bread baked in outdoor oven.

3/28

Taos. More snow. Photographing looks bleak. Treacherous dirt roads through Rio Grande National Gorge. El Rito to Abiquiu and Georgia O'Keeffe's house. Talked to Juan Hamilton, who directed us to village cemetery.

Started to Chaco Canyon on dirt road, which turned into slick mud. Did 360-degree spin down an embankment. Almost turned over. Tried another road, another 360 turn. Continued on advice of native American who said road was fine.

For 30 miles we slid around, going 5 mph, mostly downhill. It started snowing harder. Met a young couple who were stuck but who told us that the road in from the other direction was better. 22 miles and several hours later, after many stops to chop ice out of the wheel wells, we were back at the Albuquerque KOA.

3/29

Sante Fe, NM. Tea at Paul Capanigro's. He had just had his floors waxed, and brown paper runners were still down. Daisy was wild—running and sliding on the papers, jumping on the kitchen counters. We were mortified. She will not be invited back, and I'm not sure we will be either.

3/31

Amarillo, TX. Wind changed during the night and picked up to a roaring gale. Temperature dropped 20 degrees, and visibility dropped to zero because of dust storm. So this is the Texas Panhandle.

4/2

Vernon, TX. Stopped for directions—"4 stop signs," we later discovered, meant 4-way stop.

4/5

Devil's Den State Park, AR. Dyed hard-boiled eggs for Easter, using a mayonnaise jar for the dye and pages from the atlas for newspaper.

4/7

Hot Springs, AR. Excellent wax museum—VWS proclaimed Ike and Mamie Eisenhower the best she had ever seen. Outstanding chamber of horrors, featuring 14 authentic medieval tortures. I went to luxurious baths for whirlpool, steam, and hot packs.

4/8

Toledo Lake, LA. Dented and scratched the Burro on pine trees at picnic spot. Lost wheel cover. Daisy almost got run over. The dog she was playing with did, and was killed.

Disaster Cove Campground. No level campsites. Moved 3 times and finally got settled. Then water main ruptured as we started to fix dinner. Had to move again. Gathered up 400 lbs of dirty clothes and hauled them to laundry room—machines were out of commission. Found ice and tried to have a drink, but Daisy kept running figure 8s around us barking. Put her on tether. She almost hanged herself by jumping off bank into water. Gave up and turned her loose. She disappeared and we sat, somewhat shell-shocked, having a drink as the sun set over the lake. Daisy reappeared in a little while with a package of cooked spare ribs, wrapped in aluminum foil, in her mouth. After making a halfhearted effort to find their rightful owner, we ate them.

4/10
Gretna, LA. Ran out of film, so had to check into motel to develop what we had shot. Rain started during night. First heavy rain we've had in a month and luckily we were in a motel. Flood warnings.

4/11
Stuck in Gretna. Tunnel flooded, roads closed. 16 inches of rain during past 24 hours. Heaviest rain in 17 years. Intense thunder and lightning. Last of Daisy's dog food got wet. Loaded last of our film—hopefully it will see us home. This is the first time on the trip that we have had time to lie around and read and watch TV.

4/15
New Orleans. Daisy "attacked" paraplegic in wheelchair at Holt Cemetery.

4/16
New Orleans. Metairie cemetery. Ran over ground-level marker and punctured sidewall of rear tire. Bubble formed, but didn't explode until we got to nearby gas station.

4/21
Granada Lake, MS. Natchez Pilgrimage. In the campground bathroom met Elsie King, author of *Dear Smoker*, who teaches Tai Chi and has a Ph.D. in counseling and family therapy.

4/22
Memphis, TN. Warm night, marred only by Daisy's fish breath. Bought mole deterrent—a whirlygig made out of Coca-Cola cans mounted on a pole—from a man at Granada campground. The grand tusker of the trip.

4/23
Memphis. Campground owner was so impressed to have authors in her campground that she wanted to call in the press.

4/26
Paducah, KY. Daisy tore up atlas and campground guide. It must be time to head home.

4/29
Creech Holler, KY. First cem of the day, almost got stuck, mud clogged exhaust pipe. While VWS dug it out, Daisy chased chickens, geese, and ducks and almost got shot by man with rifle and only 2 teeth. When VWS tried to intervene, he swung around and almost shot her.

Camped by ourselves at Bee Bottom in Flat Gap, KY. Wind howled, fast-moving black clouds, full moon. Carloads of grizzled, toothless men kept driving through the park, circling the van, looking us over, then moving on. If we hadn't had Daisy and a gun, we would have moved on too.

4/30
Eastern Kentucky. Cemeteries here are making us feel like mountain goats. Hillsides very steep. Narrow roads with coal mines along sides. Wrecked cars acting as retaining walls. Garbage in creeks, blue steel bridges.

5/5
Nashville, TN. Went to Grand Ole Opry. Saw taping of "Fifty Years of Country Gold" (Waylon Jennings, Barbara Mandrell, Mel Tillis, Ernest Tubb, Carter Family, June and Johnny Cash, Merle Haggard, and Dennis Weaver).

5/7
Tupelo, MS. Stopped at Elvis Presley's birthplace.

5/8
Birmingham, AL. Last day out. Last shot was an empty chair. Last dinner was champagne with cheese on rye bread in Rich's parking lot.

6/28/80 — 7/28/80

6/28
Hardly out of Atlanta before one of our folding chairs blew off the top of the van. A man in a pickup truck stopped to get it (we thought for us), tossed it into his own truck, and drove off. I told VWS that was her chair.

Skidway Island, GA. Lots of bugs. Are considering mosquito netting to go over whole van.

7/1
Melbourne, FL. Temperature rising to high 90s. No AC in van.

7/3
Key West, FL. Water too warm to swim, and weather so humid that we checked into a motel. Electricity went off during the night (along with the air-conditioning). Sweltering.

7/4
Finished photographing in time to catch Wimbledon finals in the TV department of the local (air-conditioned) K Mart.

Camped at Key Largo in fancy campground by the water. Lots of trailers with lanterns shaped like owls and beer cans. Swam, watched fireworks, and lit our own array of sparklers.

7/5
Daisy came into her first heat. May have mated with ugly mutt who cooed outside van all night. Found out we had 18 more days of "heat" to endure.

Could not stay in Sarasota (no motels would take dogs) and there were no campgrounds. So we ended up hours later in

Tarpon Springs, mad and tired. It was hot, Daisy attracted dogs, and we almost got thrown out, but everyone cooled down after a swim.

7/7
Sarasota. Went to Ringling Museum. Were directed to "circus cemetery." Turned out to be Jewish (no clowns).

7/8
Callahan, FL. Did Evelyn Wood lesson #4 before leaving.

7/9
Myrtle Beach, SC. Spent morning walking on beach and reading. Headed for Marion, SC. Accidentally left tailgate of van open and my toilette article bag was lost.

Hottest day and night yet. Stopped at dozens of cemeteries and found nothing. Very discouraging.

7/11
Outer Banks, NC. Ocracoke Ferry, 2½-hour ride (23 miles), beautiful and sunny. We had railing space for sunning, reading, and throwing bread and crackers to the gulls, which they caught in midair. Looked at wild ponies through binoculars. Nice to have break from driving.

Ferry to Hatteras. Great shelling at Hatteras. Passed up numerous great camping sites because it was too early. Ended up stuck at Duck, NC. Very steep, shell-less beach.

7/12
Duck. Did what proved to be last Evelyn Wood reading practice —tape recorder died. Salted beach with reject shells. Were followed by a couple of kids who picked up every shell we dropped and kept calling, "Uncle Gus, come look what we found." No one seemed to realize we were responsible.

7/13
Burlington, NC. Camped on airstrip, behind Quonset hut. Pick-up truck got stuck, we went to help. Got covered in mud but

were finally able to pull them out with our tow chain. Missed the revival meeting in tent nearby.

7/15

Grayson Highlands State Park, VA. Camped high in Appalachian Mountains. Really cool at last. Cooked zucchini given to VWS by a pastor's wife who lived next to a cemetery where we photographed. We drank Southern Comfort and watched the crescent moon and first star come up over the mountains.

7/16

Abingdon, VA. Spent most of day in mountains, but finally had to come down to heat wave. Stayed in motel and watched Republican convention on TV.

7/19

Asheville, NC. Picnicked at Biltmore House, where Daisy drew quite a crowd. Black Mountain campground was full, so we filled our tank with water and headed down a gravel road. Found a secluded rhododendron glade next to an old wood dam which made a waterfall and swimming hole. Ranger came and told us that it wasn't a camping place, but we convinced him to make an exception.

7/20

Started over Grandfather Mountain. Took a gravel road that had a sign to a church which turned out to be many miles away. Finally pulled off road beside a stream to camp. It got so cool we could see our breath. Sat reading by the roadside until dark.

7/21

Had to put our dirty clothes back on because we hadn't washed clothes or ourselves properly for too long.

Flat tire on way down the mountain. Two fellows in a pickup came by and helped. Had to pile rocks under jack.

7/22

Brevard, NC. Stayed in ornament-filled home of two little old ladies. Daisy slept in van. Went to concert by Transylvania Symphonic Band and Wind Ensemble.

7/23

Rain cooled things even more. Drive to Highlands, NC, was delightful. Visited friends in Rabun Gap. Camped in driveway because we couldn't get up mountain to their meditation site due to wet grass.

7/27

Ellijay, GA. Temperature in the Burro has gone from an all-time high of 118 to 70.

7/28

Home at last—out of water, toilet paper, and food. For breakfast ate tomatoes left in a nearby field. Time to go home.

L. B.

ACKNOWLEDGMENTS

Special thanks to:

Patrice McDermott and Glenn Harper for temporarily forgoing their academic careers for ten years to take over the family florist business (and become our source for decoding empty picture frames and stopped clocks).

Harriet Miller for recognizing that the early photographs pointed to an uncharted world.

Dorothy Jackson for providing a carport, a dryer, and a chance to change our minds.

Michael and Jane Eisner and Sally Rich Rose Adolph Darling's housesitter (Dan Petersen) for putting us up and reminding us that it is possible to sleep in a space where you can also stand up.

Lit Simms for tending Geesil, a cantankerous, geriatric, orange-and-white cat who loved to eat and hated to be left behind.

Abby Drue for first exhibiting the work and giving us a chance to test it in front of an audience.

Michael Cornish for his early interest and for exhibiting some of the pictures in the 1981 Society for Gravestone Studies Conference at Rutgers University.

Lisa Cremin for suggesting we take the book to Aperture.

Michael Hoffman for his percipient judgment and support.

Susan Krane for being fleet-of-foot and true-of-heart.

Tom Meyer for his witty and incisive comments, suggestions, and jacket copy.

Lucinda's accountant, Simon and Schuster, and Evelyn Wood for giving us obstacles to overcome.

Jess Bell for providing a solution to the seemingly insoluble subtitle problem.

Anne Theilgard, George Battersby, Suzie Williams, Peggy Martin, and Pica the corporation cat, at Kachergis Book Design, for their enthusiastic help and patience.

And very special thanks to Joyce Kachergis for intuitively understanding the spirit of this material and designing a beautiful book that captures and communicates our feelings and intentions.